Summoned

A Breakthrough Book
University of Missouri Press
Columbia & London

Summoned

Poems by Diana Ó Hehir

University of Missouri, Columbia, Missouri 65201
Library of Congress Catalog Card Number 76–16011
Printed and bound in the United States of America

Library of Congress Cataloging in Publication Data

Ó Hehir, Diana, 1929–
     Summoned.

     (A Breakthrough book)
     I. Title
PS3565H4S9   811'.5'4   76–16011
ISBN 0–8262–0204–7

     Of the poems in this collection, "Summoned," "Imminent Earth-
quake," "A Plan to Live My Life Again," "Forgetting the Past," "A Fare-
well to the Wizard in the Wood," "Living on Death Row," "The Human
Body Is 97% Water, 3% Dust," "The Old Lady Under the Freeway,"
"A Poem for Sarah's Mother," and "Night Train" have appeared in
Poetry Northwest. "Breathing" and "The Day You Died" appeared in
kayak. "They Grow Up Too Fast, She Said" is reprinted by permission of
Poet and Critic. "Reaching the Promised Land" and "Hibernation" are
reprinted by permission of Southern Poetry Review. "News of Another
Death" is reprinted by permission of Shenandoah: The Washington and
Lee University Review. "Lady Macbeth" is reprinted by permission of
Cafe Solo. In addition, "The People in Dreams Are" and "The Outsider"
have been accepted for publication by Shenandoah; and "Desert Crossing"
and "Rubbed Stone" have been accepted for publication by Poetry
Northwest.
     "Summoned" was reprinted in Best Poems of 1973 and won the
Second Borestone Poetry Award for 1974.
     "Summoned," "Lady Macbeth," and "The Human Body Is 97%
Water, 3% Dust" were reprinted in I Had Been Hungry All the Years,
which is published by Solo Press.
     Some of these poems first appeared in a slightly different form.

For Willard, Michael, and Andrew

The Devins Award for Poetry

Summoned is the 1976–1977 winner of The Devins Award for Poetry, an annual award originally made possible by the generosity of Dr. and Mrs. Edward A. Devins of Kansas City, Missouri. Dr. Devins was former President of the Kansas City Jewish Community Center and a patron of the Center's American Poets Series. Upon the death of Dr. Edward Devins in 1974, his son, Dr. George Devins, acted to continue the Award.

Nomination for the Award is made by the University of Missouri Press from those poetry manuscripts selected by the Press for publication in a given year. In 1976, the manuscript of Diana Ó Hehir was among four selected for publication from more than 60 invited manuscript submissions and was subsequently nominated by the Press for the Devins Award.

Contents

Summoned

I

Summoned

Summoned by the frantic powers
Of total recall, sleeping pills, love;
Come down, come down, come down;
Wear red if you can, wear red
For suffering, jade for rebirth,
Diamonds in your front incisors,
A rope of orange stars—you were martyred, weren't you?
So wear a circle of gold thorns, prongs capped
In scarlet shell.

And bring with you, down, down, down,
A recollection of how you fell
Like Lucifer, morn to morn and night to night
For at least a year, your hair alight
Your rigid corpse a spoked wheel
Meteor trails ejecting from each thumb,
Sun eyes, a black light in your chest
Where the bare heart burned.

Oh, love, my love, my failure,
I can hardly bear, barely recall
The nights I ate ghosts, the nights
My shuttered, shivered window held
Three million savage stars and you;
Your spread arms splitting my sky, the light
Reflected in my own eye: your light, your might, your burn.

Come down. My sky-chart shows
Your cold corpse turning slowly, a black sun
Giving no light at all, reflecting none,
Aimlessly gentle, a twig on a pond
Circling. Gone, they say, gone, truly gone.
The eyes as blank as buttons, the mouth
Only an O. Never mind. Come down.
I can revive you. My passion is Judah, all artifice, all God.
I care with my breasts. I care with my belly's blood.
Come down.

A Poem for Sarah's Mother

"My mother was a widow. She cleaned offices.
She sent all four of us to college."—Student theme

Those evenings the offices are cold; the chill gets in under
                              your ears,
Sends an iron bar from here to here; I imagine her
Like a kind of saint hassling a dragon, a prophetess,
Toes locked against an angel on the edge of a cliff,
The angel says, prove; it says, behave.
It says, one night on a cliff is fine; afterwards
They go away, they turn your hopes inside out.
No one will remember a thing about you and your mop.

One of those fighters had to go over; one
Had to stand on its forehead in the chasm, bat hair flying.
Fall like my wishes, the mother said.
Your arms wrenched back into broken wings,
Angel. I'll wallop it out of you.

The mother is tall, her hair tied behind her ears in a kerchief.
The worst part of her day is midnight:
The tiredness of soup, sullen radio,
Sleeping children, the angel who follows after, wings akimbo,
Edges of feather dipped in paint. It has a neon line around it.
                              It says,
I'll wrestle with you, lady.

My student thinks herself an ordinary woman
Except for that battle. That's one of those childhood flashes
That startles sleep, that lights up Oakland afterward.
She says: They fought. The angel glowed like an electric heating
                              element.
They fought for fifteen years.
My mother won.

The Old Lady Under the Freeway

I've come down here to live on a bed of weeds.

Up there are white spaces with curving ceilings,
Harsh wide silver-fitted cars,
Marching squads of freckled-armed men.

My world is depths of green, a water of fern.
No one would guess that a safety hides here below,
Secretly jeweled, dropped in this special pocket.

I'm the mad old lady under the ledge. The good
Who fall headlong off the freeway bridge,
I salvage their nail files, pen knives;
I carve my way in with them;
I make a tunnel with green sides.

At night I lie on my back;
The ferns meet over my face like lover's hair.
They nestle my ear. Their words are unsafe.
The words they say are harsh and green.

I'm roasting shreds of leaf, roasting soup in a can.
My air is as solid as the inside of a honeydew melon.

The People in Dreams Are

Waiting in the dark for the dark. They're cautious as cats,
Wear soft shoes that fit the foot, know
Every stumbling place in the forest,
A hand touches there, moving a frond,

Corridors dip under the bank, the weed hangs in otter tails.
They're forest creatures, faces veined like leaves,
Eyes collecting light.

Dangerous, their palms are puddles of radium,
Their lips shine, bones are hollow;

Their waiting is a globe of water
Tensed around our dust motes, sensing
Rustles for a special ear,
Music in a hair's tension,
Fear aimless as a seedpod turning

Over the roofs of lakes, canals of pale flowers,
Out of night's swallowing eye, into a picture of
You: my love in a coat of grass disappearing into a city
                              where no one goes.

The dreams lay crumpled hands on the watcher's arm,
Steer him with a touch like mushrooms,
Like breathing.

Imminent Earthquake

The sky is as dry as baking powder.
A scuffed shoe may send the whole thing up.

Houses, sidewalks, stucco railings string out in a sound-line,
A breakable presence, garage-door magic beam.
It waits for its flag
And the rumbling mess shoves, gawky fingered, home.

Like everything you wait for.
It sits behind you holding its breath in static.
It moves in the circle of your mother's death.

Last year's earthquake: we were at the opera.
We flattened ourselves into our velvet chairs,
Clutching the arms, weighed down by that pushing apron;
A conveyor-belt roar lurched off next to my ear.
It spoke in metal of a metal world, metal people, and flowers
Clashing themselves to a brassy finish,
And death as the voice of an open gong.

Down in the works of the opera house,
Shifting weights shoved each other like cousins,
A raucous playground scraped by noise.

Afterward, the air wasn't dry. We laughed, a captive people.
We laughed as if the sea had split for us.

Cold Country

In this new chilly country where I never touch you
We travel wrapped in gray furs
Admiring the ice at the end of our breath,
The separate footsteps as distinct as cookie molds.
Branches cracking. The air drags at our voices.

There's no record on my white mind of any warm house.

Sometimes we pass by a lighted window,
People inside are having their photographs taken.
(One winter night we sat like that.
Joy pulled at my back teeth.)

Jealousy mutters against my nostrils.
Here in the cold world the windows are bank vaults.

People die of the cold! I want to say.
They're found, crouched like frogs, cuddling their rigid
shoes.
The chill then has wiped off every longing, the face is
As calm as the Snow Queen's; opaque iced eyes
Stare at a world where nothing moves.

The cold bends my throat. Beside me
There's a frozen jacket with a husband inside.

Lunar Eclipse

Whoever said yellow or said round?
Here I am fishing for the moon on my front doorstep,
Wanting to memorize it; a moon like a pulse beating at the end
                                        of a tunnel,
Moon like the gills of a white carp.

Our porch stairs are still warm. Laughter shreds over the
                                        eclipse;
The binocular in my hand is a machine
Winding us up to that open nostril
Pulling at you and me and him and her.

The sky's alive; it licks us up like milk.

We hold ourselves separate, arms slicked into seaweed;
Each of us is a pool for the other's watching.

It isn't really red, you say; that bump is the Mare Crisium.
A wedge of loneliness catches my rib. The night
Pulls a rope around my chest.

The moon beats above us,
Fleshed with veins.

Someone's Dog Has Been Hit

I want to kneel down, cradle everything in my arms, apologize
For automobiles, any human juggernauts
That toss us, crumpled, panting, by the roadway.

The dog's feet are twitching a race against time,
And my pulses, one in each wrist
Chorus, help, say, no more pain, they say
God is too far away, and the God who helps dogs
Even farther, at Sirius, the green star.

I stand, afraid to touch him.
Someone has sent for the dog ambulance.
My ribs squeeze shut on smothering; someone pour on me please
                                    a little of that
Water of life, that help that arrives with a
Roof light blinking, holds out the hypodermic needle,
Holds out a wet smoothing hand, says

Love is a man from Sirius
Who makes your feet move in a different climate, who helps you
Let go.

II

Desert Crossing

An enemy like old sins
Scratches at the base of my neck, tugs into my brain, saying,
                        loathe me;
It says: I stand like a bear on my hind legs,
My breath has the smell of roasting;
This road goes down into a valley of salt;
There are only you and me at that place, and the automobile
                        gasping like a baby.

Those hills are soft, like the lobes of the brain.
The two of us have been fighting; I've said
Things to heat the auto tires white,
Turn the gray road lumpy, spill out
Our comfort like melted lead, roll it down the sides of the gully.

Now we can sit at the bottom, draw the radiator hood over
                        our heads like a prayer shawl,
Night won't make any difference;
Hot mica, the sound of my husband's breathing, my breathing,
He has the corner of heat in his teeth;
And I have the other piece. I've lost my picture of myself
Which used to smile like my sister.

I say to myself: Change.
Loving can move over brass; it can lumber with
My creature that walks upright, arms stretched in front of its hairy
                        chest.

The Outsider

This is a meeting at which she hasn't any friends at all,
And whether or not she's me,
The woman in the long beige dress is as shrill as I am,
She lets her hair hang down in her eyes like me.

The ceiling of the room is flaked with a dark fireburst, the sign
                              of a power
With hair like branches.

And maybe it's catching; the panic
That yawns below in stress—maybe it could call for me.

Martyrdom is catching—those hands that grab my wrist as if to
                              sense pulse
Could drag me down through layers of faces
Out onto the stage, asking: burn with me.
And misery hollows out its watchers,
Leaves me with a scrap instead of belly,
Fingers empty as bladderworts hating the push from the brain,

Which still says, act:
Push the pillars down;
If the building falls against rock it may split like an iron gate,
Spilling us all out into the air.

In Mexico

I can be lonely on the edge of a riot; their many eyes
Tell me: stranger. Awkward shadows tag my feet
In their streets with the bull trotting the middle,
Over their gray stone pitted with wrongs, against their
Blood and cake, music of pewter whistle
From the armless man who dances on the corner by our hotel.

Behind it a memory: a hawk-nosed god, white-eyed:
Invader. They hung a banner across the street that said *welcome*;
It loops there still, spangled with bus fumes;
At night rockets paint the sky green and white rayon,
Colors not meant for me.

The people push quietly; they've found me out;
A woman with no daughter, no lover. Only
My white-eyed god, catching the light, sending it back in a star;

Take your foot off our tan soil, they say; take away your money, take
Your pale-colored hair.

Some of Us Are Exiles from No Land

We march into the suburbs led by a six-year-old kid
Whose only memory is the inside of a cardboard box
Where an electric light shone twenty hours a day.
He is as innocent as a white rock;
His banner carries a fringed open eye.

We don't have memories of white spaces,
Or skies with the right kind of clouds;
Our blood remembers the beat of no better sea.

Living a day at a time is easy, you others say.

You say, I do it the way my Aunty Minna did,
That old lady, crosser than most;
She wears Keds with the sides cut out;
Her nonsense gives life an arrow.

But we must invent it all: relatives out of ads,
Grandfathers shaped into American senators, a lost country
Painted by Dali.

Our army moves in on the hills like picnickers.
Watch out. We will fodder it all.
We can turn rocks into paper;
A bit of sidewalk grass becomes a green, marbled sea,
Opened for us, its chosen jewel.

Our new country will be as artful as Tashkent;
If we get there we will all be real.

The Searchers on the Beach

The animals on that beach have rheumy eyes like ours,
Pointed muzzles, gouts of terraced fur, scales
In alternating colors: blue, red, silver,
Swallowing the sun's rays;
They snuffle between the barbed wire and the weed,
Posing like beasts in the alphabet book.

Above us is the peeling building, its door choked with wire.
The clerks there pay no attention to us;
They saunter home kicking the sand ahead of them in spurts.

We turn to each other: Speak!
All that anyone wants is to be happy.
There are three children on the beach; they're as water-wise as
                                        dolphins.

Their music covers for a minute the factory's rows of windows,
The men with umbrellas who wade through clogged sand,
The whistle that waits to go off,
The water flat as a park,
The animals who know that nothing is real

Except beach
And the endless search through the dirty sand.

Night Train

Noise loops itself
Catlike, self-centered, around the walls of her bedroom,
Abrading the paper, foraging into her sleep
For nuggets of love, of wishing.
It chews them like bubble gum; it has iron teeth.
It has a shout that sends metal down into a woman's thighs;
It swaggers, matching its rhythm to the pulse in her neck.

It says, night after night your escape goes down,
You seek the wall to hold its shout.
It says: night's child.

The woman turns in the dark, touching dry linen.
There's a cricket beside the bed; she sees her husband's shadow.
The walls of the bedroom are
A cricket's cage.
Train light measures the sky; cinders are fiery needles, fiery
                              dreams.

Day comes in hot as a prairie. The trees grow scented day candles.
Silence covers the sky in blue smoke.
Everything signals that night won't come again

Except night's child. Night's favorite child
Goes down to the crossing, waves chums at the engineer.
She's seeking, still seeking in secret the coal-eyed stranger
Who drives his bright hot squawking engine through her dreams.

Across Angry Country

I want to love you again.

The country between us is a country of variance.
I'm on a swaying bridge in a windstorm; on either bank
The earthquake threatens the city; its towers lean toward
                                        the bay,
Drunkenly, like old actors.

Other people live on lighted streets; they have safe staircases,
Closets to put waiting in.
They hang windows
Over a parade of red roofs, over sunshine.

You and I are alone in our tilted world. You may be
On the top floor of the tower; you may be
In a sailboat circling hopefully on the dull water.

The point is that a facile catastrophe follows;
It waits for me to love you,
Pulling both shores with it, pulling
The tower section by section across the city,
Turning the boat upside down, its blue hull an unanswered
                                        cry for help.

Countdown

Whether it's the dry wind crowding in,
Edging its hard breath against us, pulling at the mesh of our
                                        chests,
Or maybe the early nights
Scrubbing the sky copper, forcing a line
Around hills flat as a theater backdrop,
Whatever it is, we feel edgy; our legs ache; we want to run
Down the hill in panic to the bay, throw ourselves in,
Let the cold water come up behind our ears.

You can have the house, you say, you can have
The tile-work done by the blond plumber, the photograph
Of the Mexican mountain

That floated like a white sail over the damp flat country,
Its peak pushing toward something we couldn't see.
The people that lived there knew about it; had
Stories about someone sleeping, the slopes splitting,
The air separating into flakes of color,
Landscape broken by lightning bolts, lives burnt
Into the sprawl of a new tree.

You can have the recipe for keeping moss out of the lawn.

How long have we got? Counting backwards like sky-launch,
                                        there's
A minus number until tomorrow.

Lady Macbeth

I did it for my children, did it for
An ache just above my left top rib
An emptiness, a shadow on the wall,
For those nights when the floor rocked like the roof of the forest.

I did it for a solitary walk down a moon-dry road,
My shadow yelling ahead of me,
Boredom trotting my side like an anxious dog.

My body lies to you, this bright burned hair
And quartz eyes are no more mine than the day is the wind's;
But I did it to strip them, rip them utterly

Down to a clean skull
To sharp still bleak fingers
To a rib cage enclosing air.
A hawk can scrape or fall between those sentinels,
Or a mouse industriously nurse seven thumblings.

There is no soul within them, only a carousel of blood,
A thrashing boredom. Now the arch
Of rib will open to the sky
Accepting what never rested there. I did it
To have a bird, a passionate passenger, at last within my breast.

III

For a Friend Who Lost a Part of Herself

That all of God's children must forage like this
Is understood.
We know the journey underground
Clutching the damp iced wall,
The feet nutured in fog, the hand
That craves a hand
Deducing only a stony jail.

Down at the bottom is a lake solid in glass.

Dredge it open and hack out its secrets; you'll have
The answer to all those hows,
The why of the scratch on your wrist, the sound
Of the voice that awoke you from sleeping.
You'll have what escapes everyone always, the clue
To, why did I come here before?
How could I have dropped it,
So valuable and bright a use of myself?

Coming back is the hardest; it means
Walking on wire; your aerialist's feet falter;
The floor stabs white metal; the walls crowd over
Until only the skinniest traveler can squeeze a way through
Leaving pieces as souvenirs:
Here's one from me.

There's no band waiting to meet you.
Only enough sun
To make gritty eyes blink,
To show the broken fingernail with a seam down its center,
The hand clutching what you managed to bring back.

Martyrs

The martyr that lives in me now
Nightly jams her hand in the fire,
Ignores the crowds at her rape, their jaw-frames of glass;
She draws a line through me, the American woman,
Who knows death only as something to cry over.

I had a friend who went back to Greece and was shot.
I never once thought of following him;
I was empty as a washed glass window
When we kissed on a New York street corner under the El.

Death, I felt it, was in his muscles;
Behind him were brown hills shaped like boat ramps,
Houses that had the eagle in them, black puddles on the steps, his
                                        ikon
Spread out over the sky, red-enameled.

A martyr can't love.

The martyr in me was shiny as platinum,
The rocks of her own country made the real mosaic, jewel of jewels.

While the American woman, dizzy with romance, heard
Marching headlines in the El's rattle, in the cone
Of buzzing furies coming to suck one of us in.

News of Another Death

No one can live at the bottom of a white canyon.
The canal wall has flaked scars, rusty bolts;
They go by our cabin, procession of emptiness.
There's no water under our ship;
The wall parades as high as the rest of our life.
I wake up and know it's a dream about your death.

Against the wall is the print of your palm.
And each mark takes from me. A recognition I can't make

Of dead you, damp coins across the eyelids;
Body wrapped in a web of dust-weave,
Armpits a home for cinders.
Maybe you're curved around a clay pot, gentle last gift.

And the mind as vacant as a mine shaft.
Black light, absorbing, takes all you in and swallows
Your fires, pieces of ache;
Burns to lengthen out its sky
And curves against my shell.

Your handprint a sparkle on a straight white wall
Inside of me.

The Day You Died

For Margaret, who died on a beautiful day.

The bay is
The blue of Botticelli's ocean. And you are dying.
How I hate the thought of that lustered Venus body,
And those twig-sprigged breezes bearing bright lush
Waxy roses dropping in yearning clusters;
I wish a stop of the love-lie glossing that fertile body,
A stop to the venturing feet at their shell.

Venus' feet are turned outward; she has heavenly double-jointed
toes;
Her hair uncurls like the roils of elegant packing;
Her eyes cherish an unshed secret;
Behind her scurry lamb-shaped clouds.

She is not simple. Even Botticelli's canvas
Can't contain her problem. She comes ashore

In a beginning taller than any innocence,
This daughter more natural than cloud or water,
Whose cupped hand holds the source of the river;
All questions ache behind her unstirred eyes.

While your eyes, aching, ask the corner of the room
What time it is. For you it's no time at all;
Your hours are finished, propped against the wall;
Your window closes shut upon the bay; Venus' kingdom
Fades to a squint. Inside your life
Venus' world is painted over.

Against your beaches that blue sea flows absolutely white.

Rubbed Stone

I'm afraid of the terribly good; they pray for me when my back is
                                turned,
Offer the other cheek. There's a glass shield across the back of
                                their eyes;
Their power is magic: emblem with grains of God's wing,
Hand reaching into a cloud, rubbed stone.

I fear their pale eyes, their level voices.
They're clean as metal roads, wide boned,
Calm when the wind blows, leaning
Full bosoms against the hard rail of all of us.

"I wake at night sometimes and pray for you."
Dangerous words. They open up the sky and paint a yellow stripe
                                across it,
Fetch doubts that bury me in question, leave me
Trying to be, not you, but something as implacable:
You in your wrinkled skin; the light of nights washing youth across
                                your face.

What can I do to get back at you, how rob you
Of your fierce loving weapon?

In Mexico: The Children Sell Dead Lizards by the Road

Is there a vast plain
Separating me and these Indian children,
Over it their kinds of people in skins carrying axes,
Fathers with blood-rimmed wrists,
Women who'll crunch a rabbit's scream in their teeth?

The children stare after me. Come with us, lady, I hear their eyes
                                    say.
We'll wait behind a rock, watch for blinking claws; we'll grab,
Feel the blood gout under our thumbs.

Lady, you're hungry; you're an animal
Whose only help is in your mind's landscape,
And lightning marks your mountain, a scythe flicking the sun;
Under that storm crawls man, the skinner, the fence climber.

I tell myself that there is a path up.
I had a friend once who loved me and who died;
I have a child who loves me;
Maybe it's the world's love in that hammer-shaped thunderhead;
Man creeps across his field, climbs up
Into the storm's eye:
The volt's silence, grain of light

That holds you and me; and pale-clawed creatures,
And the beautiful Indian children.

The Woman on the Shore

> "Don and I hadn't been together for
> five years, but I still loved him;
> he knew that. His last letter was to me."
> —*Interview with wife of mental patient*

Some people don't know how to waver.
Your yes was irretrievable, a bright blow
Astonishing the water. It reached out
Into crannies starred by white-thumbed fish,
Into the self's unwilling jelly.

There's no cover for such a yes; it surrounds the coral
Signaling hexagons of light.

Across those oceans of inconstant glass
He floated, face down, a jacket buoyed by air.
Only your word spread rays
Through heavy water. Your fierce
Uncompromise was his only eye.

He wrote a signature with his long dark hair:
Bye-bye love;
Drawn out by compass pole, magnet, by the frightful pull
Of resolution glittering like a colored stone,

Below where, chastening the water,
Spread out the rings of,
Margins of love.

A Plan to Live My Life Again

I would adore doing it over.

I wouldn't marry the prince and live in his Mediterranean palace;
No marble vistas of stairs, no
Peacock's tails unfurled; clematis falling from porticos;
The electric sea silent for some other feet; the lover,
Curls brushed, teeth flashing like road signs,
Holds out his arm for another fainting mate.
That glass-slipper cramps,
A slipper of notions; a little cold vise.

My other country has white roads and static skies.
Once, flashing a car across Utah, I saw
A crown of mountains upside down in the vague air;
Peaks, echoes scraping the earth,
But only in the mind's camera,
A machine as ominous
As dynamo, creasing water into electric light.

There can be no prince in such finality.
He'd blow away like a cry across white sand
End over end, his little arms flailing.
A puff in the uncanny air. Those mountains crush
Upside down, founder to all logic
A terrible problem:

Particles scraping against an interior lining.

They Grow Up Too Fast, She Said

Out under the sprinkler, naked as toads,
Popping each other face down on the grass,

I imagined her children, lemon-naked,
Jeweled in her dream like dragonflies.

My thoughts also go homeward at noon.
They climb the stairs sneaky footed
To covet a solemn face
With eyelashes like fans; they snoop into the garden
Drawing blue Xs on the children: MINE.

That woman and I would like our babies back.

We want to sag out a warm wide huddle of love
Over our children, our little warm rocks,
Solid-backed in their world fenced by light,
Under sunshine twice-powered, under bird's arms of sprinkler,
Revolving a charm to keep off the crows.

Inside those wings of safe water,
The children turn their golden backs,
They shed our pale voices, crying for time.

Headstone

    For my mother

Miles under the crust of Maryland
You're sinking at the rate of a foot a year,
Your lips carved out of earth, eyes
Faceted coals,
Your head's at my magnetic center.

Every pebble of your body is heavy, hair
Weighted strands of black rock,
Hands jet chiselings,
Your etched toes
Touch slow weighted oils that countries ride on.

When the sky turns, you turn too
Under your web of earth, a spread black rose,
Carved coin digging through steam

And down into the nub of me
Where a white lake like an eye's soft shell,
Organic, retracting, folds in home
Your smile.
("She has her hair. She has her smile exactly.")

My life's bare tree spreads out to vein the world.

Revenants

When the dead come back in dreams they do it right.

The people in my dreams always are young.
They've been living in nowhere cosseting their faces;
Their children have grown miraculously, ice-plant buds.

My friend came back in my dream, her eyes
Shiny and blue as willow plates, her laugh
Opening up old rooms in haunting houses
Where her door still speaks of her, says
I'll never stop.

The dead return in dreams with
Messages: the wash or the weather.
They tell me I'm skinny;
They smile, and my heart shatters into coke-bottle scraps.

The dead don't care.
They can walk over broken glass.

Waving Good-bye

Loving and not getting any seems good for the soul;
It makes a tough skin like the rubber on English custard,
Puts enamel on your teeth,
Fires up a machine
To hum the energy out of human touch,

Drag the warmth out of making, mash it into cubes
Blue-electric, centered by chill bubbles.
Inside each one is a hook-tailed fish of a query.

At the end of the street travels a man in a hat
Who won't come home tonight.
He climbs to the wicker seat of the ferry

Waving, good-bye, sweetheart.
Each of my thin nails bends back with love.
Take me along like your glasses; I'll be light: a paper-bag
                                        lunch.

When the foghorn moves at night it says what I mean:
All those white sounds, a trudging machine

And chill
Like a damp cord over the belly.
It jolts back to that first love that started itself without
                                        knowing
And made each empty space a silence
Just from you.

Trying to Speak

My father, filled with love clearer than winter sun,
Gropes a hand into the space I lean against.
My eyes get opaque as malachites, my belly jumps,
I see him in separate frayed pictures,
His fingertips are edged with a haze of red.

How can I talk to him?
A bird has flown into my plate-glass window.
Each of us is king of one room only.
I want to smash the crystal panel from its axis
With words to push pictures off the walls,
Mold the bird back whole

Where it beats against the deck now, a brain closing,
Its voice calling nothing to me but door squawk, twig scrape,
Sun blind,

But my father cries love, that terrible power
That wheels the west in front of our faces, turns us all seaward.

Be sensible, I say to myself, be frantic.
Nothing can change without hurting.

Forgetting the Past

The clock over the mountain strikes twelve and a half,
The hour at which all of the ladies grow up.
I am not going to worry it any more:
No more sullen sulks, no cakes untasted.
I'll forgive everything.

Behind me slovens that dark stretch of prairie,
Gritty, a road into exile, back over boredom.
It flails out under the blank sky like a cloak,
A terrible country of leisure with the sound turned off,
Under a dome where the sun sags like an eggplant,
Where the rock crashes in scalding silent dust,
Where a finger's crook takes a year, crying takes three
And feet are invisible. I walked that road searching pain with
                              my toes.

And up here the mountain is bare. Its clock has stopped striking.
I hold in my hand the egg of the morning.
The mountain reflects brightness,
And my children have packed me a lunch: six cookies,
A geranium for my hair. I tell the summit: I'm coming!
On the other side will be rocks of a different color.

A Farewell to the Wizard in the Wood

You cannot, old slow croaking aching drone
That dwells in the pit of my aptitude,
You cannot claim that it was good or that
I learned anything
Or that life was better
(No one dragged out of that mess a lesson like a captured
                        halibut)

It was bad, bad, all bad.
Its single virtue, a flashed unanimity
Neat like a bar of music, round, completed,
Phasing you off into nothing, acrid old measurer:
A puff of yellow air across yesterday's unlikely landscape.

I've paid you well; I've paid you high, don't ever try
A revisit. Bony thumbs stay out of my soup.
The four good fairies can ring my children's bed saying
                        plainsong;
You've no visiting privileges; go be a stone in the well;
Leave my fingerlings free.
I watch them tramp a way I never could;
They do not think you exist. They laugh at the idea. Good.

IV

Living on Death Row

For a correspondence student, a resident of San Quentin's Death Row.

There isn't any desertion like it.
Someone goes off and takes the key
And the human race scoots on without you.
They dash by your door saying good-bye, good-bye,
And then there is a silence like the inside of a meteor.

The jail cell spun like a question; you couldn't see the
                              sun;
The window blocked itself up with gravity;
You wedged yourself inside with your knees under your chin,
And flashed round and round. It would take your lifetime to
                              recapture earth.
Your mother died. Your father rode to Damascus where
The Department of Correction polished its amperes,
Put new bulbs in its trajectory, set off
Four rockets, all scarlet for denial. Your sister prayed
                              like mad.

No one had seen your ship for years. You inside
Thought of death as the vent of the elephant, yourself a stone.
Your sister's prayer shot by you like a blue aurora.

The warden cried, come down. But before you fell
They ransomed you. Your solitude like a cocoon, a hard
                              cloud,
Unrolled itself.
Be whole, they said. Climb out. Be new. Arise.
Out you spring shaggy as saved from hell,
An astronaut
Brought down with only a teacup more of air.

You had your pain in your arms, curved in a helmet
Over your fierce round name.
Sun polished it. You said, I am my life;
I am the dark when the squeezed eyelids make a comet;
I am my swaddled years.
I am my passage to the sun.

Hands

Somewhere in Asia, a wall
Patterned with the handprints of women,
Saint's, martyr's hands
Cased in crystal, the blood stopped up with a ruby.

My hands ache for a skill not yet invented.

It comes at me in dreams; it's all-encompassing,
A talent that will take the scars off foreheads, grow palm trees
On the salt steppes of Utah,
Hack out emblems with the powers of children;
They'll leave home, abandoning their ancestors,
Appearing in different cities with their own ways of dying.

Arbitrary as pain, that urge to make
Is edgy about time,
Imagines a monument out of wedding-cake lace,
Sloshes a picture of you across the reflecting pool, gives you
A white intense smile like a Mexican shoeshine boy's.
It draws a recognizable picture of love.

My hands remain as ordinary as mud.
They wear too many rings.
The electricity slides over them like glycerine,

When what I want is to hold the pencil
That draws a perfect circle,
A child inside it, an old man sleeping.

Reaching the Promised Land

Under my toes the grit of sand,
A row of hills, the wrong shape
But with the bulk of comfort at night.

Behind me my army, gentle crew
That has rowed across the water,
The prow of the boat is pearled, oarlocks
Green with salt wash. Hollow nubbins of seed
Trail out to the flat skyline.

I bend to touch the warm grit with both forearms,
Turn to my friends.
"Here it is. We've found it." Before

Mountains sag down. Green air comes shut like a clamshell.

That sun should have been for us; we'd haul it in
Singing songs that start: In the evening.

I think: I made this scenery out of reaching,

Out of hours when the boat squeaked like a windmill.
My friend with the blue eyes steered. My beak-nosed friend
Told raucous stories, sewed at the sail with a leather thumb.
                              I sat
On the boat seat, rowing, hedged by their stiff white linen,

Traveling hard to our scenery;
We say we are coming home to it. We never do.
The green marble sky that comes in at us fast now like a
                              wrenched plane.

Hibernation

A dream about dying.
This dying is held in a colored globe beside the water,
The waves shift heavily against it.

You can review the four corners of your life.
Here's the playground with crosspieces made of steel,
The wooden shaft that went through those hours.

Here's the man who went over the side of the wall,
His hair in ripples. The mark of his hand is
A silver print melting like salt into ice.

Here's the woman swinging by her long red hair.
Her children have gone out into the world and become famous,
They turn lead into gold,
They're more facile than the sands of the sea.

Inside this orange shell you'll sleep it all out.
Thirty-six years will drop off like strands from a palm leaf fan,
Pieces of string that the waves carry away
To knot into a new basket. Watch,

The man has turned into a flyer.
He's out over the ocean; the salt etches his wings.
His fingers grow feathers.

When you wake up you'll wave to him, flying. His heavy wings
Pulling the night from your sky.

Midwinter

For my father

Your handwriting is getting larger.
You're going backwards, winding up years, twisting them around
you,
Until, in your cocoon, you'll drop through the bottom
Onto the curved twig.

You're too small for your suit jacket now, are you dieting
To slip under the door like winter sunlight?

And you're getting younger. Flecked-brown eyes
Are blossoming out patches of blue,
Your face rounding into the face I knew in my childhood.

Last night I saw a hillside opened,
The ground turned up silver and blue for one more planting of
California wheat.
Good-bye, you said, across the backs of your eyes.

I said, I'm going to grow stronger every year,
I'll hang around your grave keeping it green
Until out you struggle like a jack-in-the-box, shiny and
tasseled, an Inca,
Your grasshopper legs heavy muscled, your hair long

To give me all your love as it springs open.

Escaping

She rips the dressings off, climbs out of the hospital window
                                 on a rope,
And onto an old black bicycle,
Shouting at the birds that rise up to scrape the air with
                                 patchwork wings,
Rides twice around the square, pedaling hard;
The bandage on her forehead glows like a new red hat.

That country is hotter than ours, along the canal
The corners of every view are red,
The sky smells of apricots,
She's letting her knees get burnt with it,
Blood tracks a question mark across her cheek.

Under the cliff, miles of still blue water, tight as a Chinese
                                 drum,
Bridges of fern heavy with plant milk, platters
Of thick white plaster flowers.

That world is shallower than ours. Behind her
The city rides on the ridge like an airborne freighter.

She'll pedal until the road winds down to a yellow track
And speckles of blood make mesh on the handlebars:
Then, down into the broad grass;

It's as hot and flat as paper
It tastes of summer.

The Old Woman Who Made Boxes

On the edge of the cliff the wind blows a typhoon;
Sand and stickers wedge in her socks, her hair blows out straight,
Stiff as a board with salt; she's clutching her tray of boxes.

Red cinnabar boxes, black jade,
Soapstone carved with birds' eyes,
A box is a cage around space.
Mad old lady in gym shoes, her days are a royal mess,
But the boxes are as elegant as the Book of Kells.

A whistle scrapes the air like jet trail;
The sea-cliff house is settling; one corner nudges the air;
Waves, bird-screams, electrical displays; it's
Land's edge for humans.

The old woman wears a brown burlap dress; the storm
Tucks it tight at her bony knees, into her V;
Wave froth frosts her shins like the storm-king's beard.
She thinks: soapstone bird eyes, red jade with a grape at the
                            center;

I've made a hedge of Byzantine ovals;
They'll cut the wind.

Breathing

I've been struck by lightning only once.
It soaks you down, dissolves the bones to soup,
Rattles your eyes like castanets.

The hands of lightning wrap you in plastic sheets,
You're the child inside, pulling.
Don't breathe, little one. Lie still.
Love, what comes out of lightning? Power,
A passion to breathe, even when breathing's death.

It happened only once. Life now is different.
Roads are straight as curtain rods; it's easy
To get up in the morning; the gardener squeaks his rake along
                              the walk;
The mail is tied in bundles. I can help you.

Sometimes I meet someone in the supermarket; in her eye
The back gone out of the pupil, specks of mica, blackness
Where light has wedged a window into spiky country.

We watch each other, sharing a past:
Lightning. The taste of lightning.

The Watcher

The zealot that sleeps in my bed is made of stone
Like a Catholic saint. Her marble eyes
Adjusted open by two splayed fingers, their pupil slots
Counting things. She has made a map
Of her death, knows where everyone will stand,
What weapon will open her skull.

The zealot is brusque about sleeping. Only my songs can soothe her.
Death in some kind of glory
Is all that moves in her garden
Over the trampled grass, the ring of listeners,
Her unloosened marble legs.

No kin of mine, she weighs down my bed
Taking up room that might have been warmed by a sister.

When I lie against her
Her open eyes touch a cut on my lips
And the gift of speech comes like water;
I can talk about endings,
She falls asleep, sharp like the ridge of a house
And I drop off of her into my own landscape.

It's wilder than hers, if only she knew.
My own circle of grass
Is a green so high it floods out my sky with motion.

The Human Body Is 97% Water, 3% Dust

The dust must be dumped to await the Hoover Co.,
That water circles the universe twice, comes back
Intent on becoming part of someone great.

Next time, let me be someone brave,
Someone fanatically true, someone whose heart
Expands like an old-fashioned suitcase,
Someone who knows that everything is real.

I know a lady whom nature gypped wholesale;
She's angled like King Tut in her chair,
And no one ever thinks of her as petitioner, only as motion,
Or as a Saracen passion, or as four fields at evening
When day rises and sovereignty moves in.

Protest gets no place. One could turn the whole sky out
                    by its corners,
Shake loose the fabric of being;
Still, some other comet again will some day be trapped thus,
Trapped, tricked, caged in the deep hole in the mountain
Where incandescence brighter than emphasis glows from the
                    stones at our feet,
The walls we hesitate to touch.

But, friend, they have promised me absolutely,
(They have written it up in a book) that next time will be
                    better;
You will speed on new ski blades. I don't know
What I want for myself. It seems logical, it seems true
That spirit steals from sense, joy is rationed. So instead
Of the unimpeachable body, the perfect mind, I'll take
                    your present fetch, your kind;
Tracks in the soul's snow only, trails
In the soul's bright snow.